I0493054

First Page On The Search Engines

ALUN HILL

Alun Hill - Talking About Business

Contents

Why The First Page On The Search Engines?   v

1. Why Do Businesses Need SEO?   1

2. On-Site SEO Versus Offsite SEO   5

3. Basic Elements Of Onsite SEO: Content   9

4. Basic Elements of Onsite SEO: Keyword   17
    Research

5. Basic Elements Of Onsite SEO: HTML   25

6. Basic Elements Of Onsite SEO: Site   31
    Architecture

7. Basic Elements Of Off-Page SEO: Trust   37

8. Basic Elements of Off-Page SEO: Links   43

9. Basic Elements of Off-page SEO: Personal   49
    Factors

10. Basic Elements Of Off-page SEO: Social Media   55

11. Local SEO   61

Why The First Page On The Search Engines?

Rarely does anyone browse through the search results after the third page.

Even among the first three pages, users don't give them equal priority, 94% of them click on links presented on the first page, slightly less than 6% click on links shown on the second page, and a very small percentage on the links displayed on the third page.

33% of all traffic goes to the first link on the first page, and that is why a lot of websites aspire to get in this position.

There is a joke in SEO circles that the best place to hide a dead body would be the second page of Google – as no one ever looks there ....

FirstPageOnThe SearchEngines.com

CHAPTER 1

Why Do Businesses Need SEO?

In this world of internet marketing, you are bound to hear or come across certain terms like e-commerce or big data.

Among those terms, there's one that's probably heard more than others.

Yes. We're talking about SEO or Search Engine Optimization.

Whether you're part of a large business or a small one, chances are that you've heard about SEO during every meeting and brainstorming session. You've probably received calls or e-mails asking you to sign up for an SEO service or some sort of SEO advice.

Now, that brings us to the question of why this "SEO" thing is such a big deal. Well, truth be told, SEO has its benefits.

In fact, these benefits are very significant and they can play a direct role in helping your business grow. As long as the world of online or internet-based business exists, SEO will continue to play a central role in helping these businesses stay afloat.

So, here are a few reasons as to why you should really take the SEO thing seriously.

Excellent ROI

In order to understand how SEO can deliver high ROI, let us first understand how SEO works.

In a nutshell, SEO involves using certain techniques to make your website as much visible as possible among the barrage of other websites on the internet.

In today's online business world, the "website visibility" we just mentioned, matters a lot. After all, people can only buy from you if they know that you exist and in order to make sure that people know you exist, you need to market your website. SEO is one of the ways in which you can market your website.

By using tactics such as keyword optimization, you make it easier for search engines to find your site and deliver them in the first few search results. To put it simply, when a person searches using the exact keywords, your site is bound to show up among the first 10 results. In turn, that increases the chances of your site being accessed and the person turning into a potential lead and eventually, a customer.

Your Site Becomes User-Friendly

SEO also helps your site become user-friendly. SEO isn't just about getting your site to show up in the top search results. It's also about making the site easy to use and navigate through. SEO is user-focused and how a customer feels about your site does have an impact on your rankings. So, you could say that a happy user makes search engines happy too.

For instance, using good on-page SEO techniques makes it easier for search engines to go through and make sense of the content on the website. The same benefit is enjoyed by the user of the website as well. So, SEO makes your site user-friendly and search engine friendly.

When users like your site, they are going to give you all their attention and that boosts your search engine rankings. See the connection here?

Better Conversion Rates

Apart from boosting the incoming traffic to your site, SEO can also help boost conversion rates. Traffic and conversion rates are related. In fact, they are directly proportional. It's not that hard to understand. The more traffic you have, the higher the conversion rates are bound to be.

When we say conversion rates, we are referring to the number of users who respond to your CTA (Call to Action). In other words, these are the users who actually buy your services or products. They aren't just here to look around.

So, when your user traffic is really high, there are bound to be more buyers.

Therefore, it would be safe to say that SEO contributes directly to your revenue.

Branding

SEO can also help you create a brand and that's important because people trust brands. SEO involves using the right keywords. However, these keywords don't just attract traffic. They also describe and define your business image. The words you use to sell your products or services speak volumes about your brand's identity.

So, by using content that is keyword rich and also descriptive of your business, you create more traffic and also, unique brand identity or image. Once you create that brand identity or image, it becomes easier to stand out from the crowd.

Access To Customer Data

SEO also helps you understand your customers by providing you with all kinds of data. For instance, there are SEO analysis tools that tell you how a user found your site and what they are looking for. In other words, you can get a clear picture of how each user behaves and this can help you optimize your site further to match the expectations of potential customers.

Cost-Effective Advertisement

SEO is probably the most cost-effective way to market your business. Marketing your business in the traditional way is bound to burn a hole in your pocket. Let's face it. Traditional advertising isn't cheap or for that matter, even pay-per-click advertising can turn out to be extremely expensive, especially if those clicks aren't really converting.

SEO, on the other hand, is all about optimizing your website to bring in more traffic. It's something you can do yourself without spending any money. Even if you were to hire a SEO service, you would still pay fees that are a pittance compared to what you would spend on pay-per-click advertising or traditional advertising.

CHAPTER 2

On-Site SEO Versus Offsite SEO

There are primarily two kinds of SEO techniques. One's called 'On-Site' SEO and the other's called 'Off-Site' SEO. So, what are they and what's the difference between these two? Well, let's take a look.

On-Site SEO

On-Site SEO is the SEO technique or method that most of us have heard about. This is the most basic SEO method and whenever you hear someone discuss about SEO, On-Site SEO is what they are most likely referring to.

On-Site SEO deals with optimizing your website's content, titles, tags, meta-data and pretty much every single aspect of your website's structure around the necessary keywords.

It's a very straightforward SEO method. All you need to do is identify the keywords that are relevant to your business and are most likely to be used by your target audience. Once you do that, you need to determine search volume and pit it against the competition. The final step involves creating high quality content around those chosen keywords.

You have to ensure that your website content has enough of those keywords. Plus, you have to also make sure that the quality of the content isn't compromised just to make room for keywords.

Plus, it's not enough to insert keywords into the primary content. Keywords must also be inserted into the website's metadata such as meta-tags, URLs, image tags, and meta-descriptions.

This is pretty much what On-Site SEO is all about. There is very little you can do beyond this except keep updating your keyword strategy on a periodic basis and creating unique and useful content.

The results of your efforts beyond this point are left in the control of search engines such as Google, Yahoo or Bing. These search engines will index your site and rank them accordingly, Of course, you could provide search engines with a site map and request for indexing, but that takes around 3 months anyway.

Other than that, the only option left is to add more pages with keyword-optimized content. By adding more pages, you are providing search engines with more indexable and searchable content.

Off-Site SEO

Off-Site SEO is where things get trickier because this particular SEO method isn't as straightforward as On-Site SEO and requires consistent and constant effort.

Before you get a picture of Off-Site SEO, you need to know certain things about search engines and how they rank websites. You see, it's not just keywords that help search engines find or rank your website. Search engines also rank your website based on trustworthiness and quality.

The parameter that search engines follow to determine this involves looking at other sites that link back to your site. When there are a large number of websites that provide links to your site, then it tells the search engine that your website is an authority on a particular topic and a respected one at that.

Plus, if an already respectable site links back to yours, then that can really boost your search engine rankings. For instance, if CNN adds links to your site within its own content, then that means that your site is a source of reliable information and search engines will pick up on this. Eventually, they'll start to promote you by ranking your web pages higher.

By the way, the links that direct users to your site are referred to as 'backlinks'. So, now, the question is how do you generate backlinks?

Well, for starters, you can begin by publishing press releases about your business, products or services. These releases need to be keyword optimized and peppered with links back to your website. Then, you will have to get your press releases published in major PR portals like Business Wire or PR Newswire. These PR portals will further publish your press release in other major news outlets.

So, what starts to happen now is that your content becomes visible on major websites and the users accessing those websites to read your press release will start to click the backlinks on your press release, which will bring them to your website.

Are You Starting To See A Pattern Here?

Similarly, there are other methods to generate backlinks. For instance, you could try guest blogging.

Guest blogging involves writing blogs on topics that are relevant to your own business. However, in order for guest blogging to be effective, you will need to reach out to blog sites that already have a high ranking and cater to your specific industry. Luckily, they aren't that hard to find. Just go to Google and type in "guest blogs" along with the name of your industry such as "automobiles". You'll end up with several links to guest blog sites that are specific to your industry.

Plus, guest blog editors are always looking to find more content for their blog sites. So, you shouldn't have a hard time convincing them to publish your blogs.

So, when it comes to the topic of On-Site vs. Off-Site SEO, there is no single winner.

You need to implement both these tactics to make sure your website is noticed. Relying on a single SEO method will fail to produce the results you're looking for.

CHAPTER 3

Basic Elements Of Onsite SEO: Content

Why Is Content King?

Content is king because of how much the internet has penetrated our daily lives.

With a billion sites scattered over the Web, search engines sift through them, index them according to their content, and serve up results when someone queries using a particular keyword or a set of keywords. Although Google, Bing, Yahoo! and other search engines list almost all the sites relevant to a query, they are not displayed at random, but rather in an orderly fashion – the ones with the most relevant content get displayed first.

And so there is always a mad rush to get to the top of the rankings, or at least the first page. This, in essence, is the objective of SEO or Search Engine Optimization, as it has been seen that very few people go beyond the third page of search results.

Search engines are not humans and so cannot compare sites when they have different design elements. One site may have some breathtaking design with some top-notch images, while another may be basic. Ideally, the former should be ranked above the latter, but search engines look for a comparable quality so that they can indeed rate them on that parameter.

The only (the only one, mind you) comparable quality/design element is text. And the sites which provide more textual information are thus ranked higher.

This is the reason why Wikipedia pages are usually ranked #1 for a particular keyword when the search results are shown – Wikipedia pages are not great at design, by any stretch of imagination, but they are rich in textual content and this is what causes them to be generally at the top in search engine rankings.

For quite some time, unscrupulous web designers manipulated their pages into the top search results by stuffing keywords – a single keyword would be repeated several hundred or thousand times on the webpage so that search engines would pick it up and think with all these references, the page was rich in information pertaining to that keyword.

The keywords would be cleverly hidden using elements of web design, such as the color of the text being the same as the background, and so visitors to the site wouldn't think anything was odd or out of place.

But without quality content, search engines showing these pages in the top results served no real purpose to users, so they modified their algorithms accordingly.

Today, a more accurate version of 'Content is king' would be 'Quality content is king'.

How Is Quality Content Defined?

Quality content is simply that which adds value in some way. While this is subjective, it could be said to add value if it checks one of the following boxes:

• Does it solve a problem?

• Does it provide the answer to a question?

• Is it entertaining?

- Is it capable of making people laugh?

- Has some unique, expert insight been offered?

How Does Google View Quality Content?
This is truly the million-dollar question. It could literally generate millions of dollars in revenue if your site is ranked by Google and deemed worthy to be placed at the top.

Some of the ways Google ranks your page are as follows:

Multimedia: If there are YouTube videos, your page is likely to be ranked higher by Google, which also looks at the number of links present on a page. Page videos, images and infographics might not have links associated with them, but what they do is make the content easier to understand. This results in a greater likelihood of your page being shared on social media (up to 12 times higher than a text-only webpage) – and that is good for the rankings. Facebook likes for the page too work like a charm. Reliable sites that link to your page are also great when it comes to improving page rankings.

Content Length: Google tends to reward pages that comprehensively cover a topic or subject. Wikipedia is still the gold standard here. If you want your page to be ranked highly, consider having 1000 words or more.

But then again, it is estimated that 30-50% of internet access happens on mobile devices. A page containing such a large amount of text may be too much to consume for those using such devices, and may subsequently earn lesser shares on social media than a page of reduced word length. So the trick is to identify your target audience segment, and write for them, without thinking about how it will be ranked by Google. You don't have to worry, because Google rewards quality content. Wikipedia is still the example – its pages aren't written for Google. A page may still be rated highly by the search engine even though it may contain only 200-250 words.

Grammar, Spelling And Punctuation: Interestingly, this

figures into the rankings as well. Well-written, quality-checked content that is laid out in an easy-to-understand manner (Google also looks at content layout and whether it elucidates the concept or befuddles the reader, so page formatting is just as important) scores more points than a rant. Now you know why blogs don't really make it into the top search results.

A site's design may be great, but if the content is spread all over the page, don't expect Google's search algorithm to act like a human. Even if there are multiple authors, enforcing editorial standards across the page or site helps.

Readability: If your page is aimed at children or those for whom English is not a first language, a high reading level (there are tools to measure this, such as Flesch-Kincaid) causes your page to drop in the rankings.

Author's Level Of Expertise: There are some pages that Google terms YMYL or Your Money, Your Life. These have to do with personal finance/investing or health, both physical and mental. Google looks at the author, whether he/she holds the necessary level of expertise, as indicated by his/her academic degrees and/or job profile, whether he/she has written other articles, and ranks accordingly – being careless with this could lead to people losing their health and/or money, both of which are very important.

Publishing Domain: Something that is published on a more trustworthy domain, like that of a news portal, is bound to be ranked more highly than the same content on a less-reliable domain like BuzzFeed.

Comments: Pages for which comments are enabled have a higher ranking, and as a follow up to this, the number of comments and the quality of comments work their magic together (a high number of low quality comments, such as those containing spam links, or those which are abusive and/or do not contribute to the discussion in any way, does not help). What Google looks at the number of comments the page has generated, and whether or not these add to the conversation positively by offering additional knowledge that is not present on the page.

How To Create Great Content?

Now that you know what quality content is and how Google views it, here are a few tips to ensuring that the content on your page is as good as it can be

- See to it that the YouTube videos are relevant to the content (Google finds this out from what genre/category it has been published in, its title, meta description, length of video, tags, user comments et al), and not some random pick just for the sake of improving ratings. Even if you leave Google out of it, how would your users react to irrelevant or barely relevant videos?

- Get the content proof-read by a professional for grammatical mistakes and/or typographical errors. These are best avoided – it is a pain going through poor writing. Even If your page was ranked #1, how would users feel about you if the content on your page was full of spelling mistakes? What kind of professionalism would that convey?

- Rewrite the content so that it is at a lower reading level, especially if you expect those who read it not to have a high level of education or proficiency in English – a site or page offering legal advice on immigrating to the United States, for instance, is unlikely to have native speakers of English as its readers.

- If you cannot have a recognized expert write for you, the content can still be made to appear more credible by including direct quotes of such experts on the subject. These have to be relevant, of course, and it helps to include their full names and designations (past or present). Even if direct quotes look out of place on the page, indirect quotes are still a good bet.

- To achieve greater visibility for your content, use a reputed site which accepts quality articles from users. The Huffington Post is a portal where people can submit their contributions. Because it is primarily a news portal, there is that integrity which gets added to your content.

 People love experts who are willing to share their knowledge with others. Publishing quality content gets you seen as an expert on the matter.

When you identify yourself as being associated with a company (most sites of the above kind also have a short one-line description about the author, usually the position held at an organization), that also translates to interest in your company/organization, which can be good for business.

- Moderate the comments, if possible, to ensure that only quality comments which add value are published on the page/site.

Why Freshness Of Content Is Important – And How Can You Keep Your Site/Blog Content Up-To-Date?

Google constantly crawls the web, looking for new/fresh content. This is how a news article can be indexed and added to Google's search results in less than a minute. If you keep the content 'stale', there is bound to be a drop in traffic and your page/site gets pushed down the order, just like how old news articles are hardly seen in the rankings.

"But mine is a company website. Does that mean I have to keep refreshing the content every two weeks?"

Yes and no.

It is highly unlikely that a company would need to keep changing the content on its site regularly – this also sends out the wrong impression to clients – but it can indeed update its site without changing the content.

This is done by adding fresh content to the website. Again, this poses the same problem, as the values of a company are expected to be the same and not subject to change, but instead of adding content to the main pages, fresh content can be added to a blog section. Updates about the company in the form of blog posts should suffice to convince Google that the content on your site is not outdated.

Another SEO trick is to publish a snippet of a blog on social media and then ask followers to read more of it on the site.

This social media traffic to your site is very helpful for the rankings. If blogs about a company cannot be published, say every week, but only once in two weeks or a month, some choose to first publish it on the site, then wait for another week or two before they publish a snippet of the blog on social media.

This way, Google stays interested because first there is new content to be indexed, and then there is enough social media traffic (this kind is associated with real users and not bots, so it is the real deal) to keep your site steady in the rankings. Throw in multiple social media platforms into the mix, time your blog snippet + Read more at link activity on them right and you have an intelligent SEO strategy on your hands even with limited content.

Direct Answers:

One of the more recent updates provides searchers with direct answers. If your content is written clearly enough for Google to recognize it as an answer to a particular question, it will show up directly beneath the search bar.

This is a new feature and Google calls it the Quick Answer box.

When a user keys in a query (Google recognizes this from the 5 Ws and 1 H, or rather one of "who, what, where, when, why or how"), the rest of the question is scanned for keywords and surprisingly, a direct answer is presented in a box above the search results.

This also has the link to the page, and the date the content was originally published.

It can be a great way of getting traffic to your site – and not just any, these are genuinely interested users and so are likely to spend some time on your page.

There are several sites/pages out there that provide the same information.

To ensure that it is content from your page that gets shown in the Quick Answer box, there really is only one way – the content should be of high quality and your page/site should be trustworthy, which is a direct result of not manipulating it for search engine indexing, but publishing it for the original purpose the World Wide Web had intended – sharing information as much as possible, in the best way you can.

CHAPTER 4

Basic Elements of Onsite SEO: Keyword Research

What Is Keyword Research?

Keyword research refers to the practice of identifying and determining ideal search terms used by people when searching for a particular item or topic on the internet through search engines.

To put it as simply as possible, keyword research helps SEO (Search Engine Optimization) professionals find the words that are most likely to be used as search terms by their target audience.

When the ideal set of keywords is identified, SEO professionals and website developers can develop content around those keywords. This helps them make their websites more visible and rank higher as far as organic search results are concerned.

Even the identification of a niche keyword is enough to help SEO professionals determine the other keywords that their target audience is most likely to implement in their searches.

Keyword research is carried out with the help of specialized tools called 'keyword suggestion' tools.

An example of a popular keyword suggestion tool is 'Google

Adwords Keyword Planner', which not only provides keyword suggestions, but also functions as a thesaurus.

Keyword suggestions are also provided by the search engines themselves, along with the number of searches for each of those keywords.

This kind of information is collected by SEO professionals and used to pick out specific keywords that are relevant to their website's SEO objectives.

In Google, 20 to 25% of searches comprise particular long tail keywords. Ranking these keywords is a fairly easy task as long as you have an optimum amount of content and backlinks to go with them.

Keyword research is an important part of internet marketing and it helps businesses achieve a high return on investment.

Why Is Keyword Research Important?

The primary aim of keyword research is to find and generate a large volume of keywords that are relevant to the search terms used by a website's target audience. Of course, keyword research involves a lot of precise effort.

The general method used in keyword research involves the use of keyword suggestion tools and hours of brainstorming.

In order to receive the best results, an obvious requirement is to find the most relevant keywords. At the same time, it is also necessary to make sure that these keywords are used as high volume search terms and have very little competition.

The lower the competition, the easier it becomes to get a high search engine ranking and a better search volume. This, in turn, provides a high amount of incoming traffic to the website.

However, there is a disadvantage to this strategy. It has been observed that keywords with low competition have very low search volumes. On the other hand, high volume search terms have keywords that are hard to rank.

There are three things to consider when executing a keyword

research. Firstly, useful keywords are always related to the content and theme of the website.

Keywords that are not relevant to a website's content are usually blocked by search engine algorithms. Useful keywords with high levels of competition usually have a very low ranking, while keywords with low volume searches do not add to a website's traffic and therefore, are pretty useless in terms of SEO.

For instance, one of the most popular and highly competitive keywords used as a search term in Google is "making money".

There are almost 3000,000,000 searches done using these keywords. What that means is, there are over a million websites who are competing for these keywords.

So, when SEO professionals start researching keywords, they need to find keywords that are relevant to the term "making money".

So, that would bring them to search terms such as "acquiring money", which has a much lower search volume. In fact, there are only 47,900,000 million searches conducted with the keywords "acquiring money".

Another way to improve traffic is to go for very specific keywords such as "making money in Texas". Specific keywords tend to be less competitive and they usually have a relatively higher ranking.

There are multiple tools that help with identifying keywords and analyzing them.

For example, as mentioned earlier, one such tool is Google Adword Keyword Planner. However, the keywords suggested by this tool are exclusive to Google searches only. This tool can provide SEO professionals with keyword traffic estimates, generate newer keywords by combining other keywords, and provide variations of existing keywords.

The Use Of Keywords Has Become More About Semantics
In recent times, there have been some changes in the way

keywords play a role in SEO. Of course, keywords still play a very significant role in boosting the effectiveness of internet marketing campaigns.

However, the connection between a website's visibility and keywords is more complex now. There are several other considerations to be made when indulging in Search Engine Optimization.

Keywords are still needed by Google to make sense of a website. But, these keywords just function as minor pieces of data to help simplify Google's analysis. They really don't play a big role as far as real rankings are concerned.

In other words, how you place your keywords matters more than how much you use them. For example, if you're an automotive services website, then placing the words "automotive repairs" in your title tag has a better effect than inserting those words into the content body in large volumes.

Search engines, especially Google, index your website by prioritizing certain areas.

Headers and metadata take up the highest priority, while body copy takes up secondary priority. Footers and side bars are the last areas to be considered.

So, when it comes to the high priority areas, it's advisable to insert details about your company or business. However, don't rely on just using keyword phrases. That could actually make your site look repetitive and affect your rankings in a negative way.

Also, Google has stated to focus more on meaning than on just plain words. When Google indexes your site, it doesn't just look for keywords anymore in order to match them with search queries.

Instead, it adds another approach. Google tries to make sense of the information on your website to determine what it really offers and what it's all about. So, you could say that

Google has become much smarter than it used to be. Way smarter.

In fact, Google's very own study found that almost 70 percent of its search results are based on derived meaning. What that means is you can be put under the same category no matter how many relevant keywords you use or how often you use them.

So, your optimization must be focused on creating meaning and not just on keyword use. In fact, you can even avoid keyword usage altogether and start prioritizing high quality content in order to establish yourself as an authority on a particular subject.

Another interesting change that is occurring in the field of SEO is semantic searches. What this means is that Google can now derive meaning not just from your keywords, but also from user searches. In other words, Google can now predict what the user is specifically searching for.

For instance, in the past, Google depended on keywords to provide relevant search results.

So, if you entered "cheap restaurants in Texas", then Google would scan the web to hunt for websites that displayed content with those exact keywords or keywords that were relevant to those search terms. So, a user could end up with all kinds of results as long as the website had those exact keywords.

Now, Google uses 'semantic search', which was released as part of the Hummingbird upgrade in 2013. So, what semantic search does for Google now is that it helps the search engine provide results that are even more specific.

If you were to search for "cheap restaurants in Texas" in Google today, you would get search results that would show exactly that.

So, if your website has content that indicates that you're restaurant is in Texas and offers an inexpensive menu, then your website has a high chance of popping up right on top of all the search results. The point here being, content is even more significant than keywords.

The Do's And Don'ts Of Keyword Usage

Here is a list of keyword dos and don'ts to make your SEO efforts more effective.

1. **The Do's**

- Use keywords in the <title> tag. The <title> tag is an important part of your website's structure. It is the first thing that pops up in the search results. Ideally, you need to insert a keyword right at the start of the <title> tag.

- Use keywords in the URL. Keywords in the URL provide an extra advantage. Try using hyphenation to separate the keywords in order to make them more identifiable for search engines.

- Use an optimum amount of keywords. Too many keywords will ruin the quality of your content and content quality matters in terms of website ranking. To little will cause your website to lose visibility.

- Add keywords to headings (H1, H2 and H3). Headings are a high priority area for search engines. That's the first thing they look at.

- Insert keywords into your start age. Search engines use a top-down approach so having keywords placed in your first pages will have an impact.

2. **Don'ts**

- Avoid spelling errors. Using wrongly spelled words will actually provide you with an abundance of keywords. However, they will ruin the quality of your website. So, if you do need to use misspelt keywords, use them in the meta-tags.

- Avoid diluting your keywords. Stop inserting too many keywords into the content. This will distract the search engines from the primary keywords. Focus on what the most important keywords; the ones that are most relevant.

- Avoid keyword stuffing. Using the same keywords over and over again affects the credibility of your content. In fact, search engines are programmed to sniff this tactic out and they often ban websites that do this.

CHAPTER 5

Basic Elements Of Onsite SEO: HTML

Title Tags

Title tags, as mentioned earlier, are very important for your SEO strategy. Title tags are part of your website's meta-data. Meta-data refers to the XHTML or HTML elements that offer search engines information about your website.

These elements must be positioned as headings in your HTML document. The Title Tag is one such element. You'll find them right at the top of your HTML document in the area marked as <head>.

Title tags function like the chapter heading for a book. They basically let users know what your site is all about.

So, it would be logical to say that your title tags can either convince a user to visit your site or avoid it based on how well they are written.

A simple motto used in title tag development is that they should be written for humans and formatted for search engines.

A tile tag looks something like this in your HTML document: <title>Welcome to Tony's Automotive Repairs<title>

In the search results, they appear as the blue-collared

clickable links and in some browsers, you'll find them right at the top, in the browser bar.

While developing title tags, there are a few things that require attention. For starters, title tags shouldn't be too lengthy or too short.

Ideally, 70 characters is the suggested length. Similarly, it is best to insert the primary keywords in the beginning of the title tag and the other keywords towards the end.

Also, it is necessary to separate keywords in order to make them readable. The best way to do this is by inserting pipes. So, instead of writing "cars and bikes", you can write the keywords as "cars|bikes".

Avoid using commas, dashes, or underscores.

Keep things simple. Omit words that make your title tags look like complete sentences. Also, each page must have a separate title tag and it must be relevant to the content on the specific page.

You must also never forget to include the company or business name in the title tag. You can either put it right in front or at the end, depending on relevance and importance.

Sometimes, Google will try to change your title tags if it feels that they don't meet the standards. So, try to meet the standards as much as possible by following the above mentioned suggestions. That's your only defence

Meta-Descriptions

The primary purpose of meta-descriptions is to improve the click-through rate. These are the short descriptions that you find right below the title tags and they do play a role in your SEO strategy. So, the way you write them can have an impact on whether your title tags are clicked or not.

Here are a few ways in which you can improve your meta-descriptions.

• Keep an eye on the characters. Ideally, meta-descriptions

should be no longer than 155 characters and no shorter than 130 characters. However, the number of characters you use may vary depending on how much relevant content you need to show. So, finding long meta-descriptions isn't that uncommon.

- Meta-descriptions should be actionable. These are words put together to make your site as attractive as possible. Users should be tempted to click your title tag after reading the meta-description. So, try to make your meta-description look like a 'call to action'.

- The content in meta-descriptions should be structured. For instance, include primary details about your product or service. If a user is looking for a specific product, your meta-description can convince them to click, if there are a fair bit of details.

- Use relevant keywords. Once again, keywords come into the picture and they have an impact on the effectiveness of your meta-description. If there are relevant keywords in your meta-description, Google just might prioritize it in the search results.

- Meta-descriptions for each page must be unique. Using the same meta-description can affect Google's user experience. If you don't have anything unique to put up, just leave the meta-description empty. Google will use snippets from your page content to create its own meta-description.

Schema

You've probably never heard of the term 'Schema', in the context of SEO. However, it's one of the latest things to pop up in this arena and is basically related to the concept of 'semantic searches' we discussed earlier.

The primary purpose of Schema Markup is to help search engines derive meaning from your content. Basically, Schema

Markup helps search engines differentiate between simple keywords and real meaning.

For example, if you were to search using the keywords "Jeffrey Archer" normally, Google would provide you links to every possible website that has the words "Jeffrey Archer" inserted into its content. So, you would end up with links to random sites that have nothing to do with the famous author.

However, with Schema Markup, Google can now identify sites that are actually about the author. To put it simply, the search results are much more specific.

This is something that benefits users and website owners.

On the whole, it gives your website a better chance to achieve a higher ranking because you can now direct users specifically to your site, provided the content in your site is what the user is looking for in the first place.

You can provide Schema Markups for all kinds of content including articles, restaurants, movies, TV shoes and events etc.

So, how is this done? Well, it's actually quite easy. Here are the steps you need to follow.

- The first step is to go to Google's Structured Data Markup Helper.

- Then select the data type you want to markup. You can find several options here.

- Once you select the data type, add the URL link to your page in the space below. You can also just post the HTML.

- Now, the page, whose link you just entered, will start to load in the markup tool. This will lead you to the 'tagging items' workspace. Here, you'll find your web page and the data items. The former on the left pane and the latter on the right pane.

- Select the elements you want to markup. Whichever element you select will be added to the data items. However, you can't add more than a certain number of elements. So, just add the most important ones.

- Now, create the HTML by clicking the 'Create HTML' button.

- The next page will display the HTML version of your page. Here, you will find all the micro-data inserted in the selected areas.

- Now, the next step is to add Schema Markup to your whole web page. For this, you will either have to access your source code or your CMS (Content Management System). Once you're there, just place the highlighted snippets in the right spots. The schema markup code can be found through the yellow markers which appear on the scrollbar.

- Now click finish. You will notice a pop-up that displays a series of "Next Steps". Among these steps, you can click the one that says "Test Your Structured Data". This will give you a preview of what your page might look like with all the markups. Here, you can paste the generated code, which is downloadable. After you paste the code and click "Preview", the tool will show you what your content will look like in the search results provided by Google.

This is just a basic introduction to Schema Markup. To get a more in-depth view of how it works, please visit Schema.org.

Subheads

The thing about users who log onto sites is that they do not actually read your content. Well, at least not immediately. The first thing they do is scan the content.

This is because they're basically trying to find the information that matters most to them. This is where subheads come into the picture. Subheads make it easier for users to spot the information they really want.

That's why it's important to create emphasis around subheads. Subheads are a core part of your SEO strategy.

By using <H2> tags with your subheads, you're telling search engines that the content under your subhead is important or relevant and it has some value to offer.

So, when you craft sub-heads make sure you follow some of the standard SEO rules.

For starters, your subheads must have the relevant keywords inserted in them.

However, do it only when it matters. Pointless keyword insertions, especially in the subheads, will just make things look bad.

Also, make sure your subheads are a natural part of the content progression.

Apart from attracting the user's initial attention, your subheads must also convince them to go back and read the entire "story".

CHAPTER 6

Basic Elements Of Onsite SEO: Site Architecture

Another significant aspect of SEO success is site architecture.

So, what is site architecture?

Well, website architecture refers to the overall design, usability, aesthetic value and functionality of the website. To put it simply, your website needs to look good, be user-friendly and also, efficient. Good website architecture can have a positive impact on your SEO efforts.

In order to achieve good website architecture, you need to focus on areas such as content, navigation, interactive capabilities of the site, business plan and information architecture etc.

Here is a list of all the factors that play a role in creating high quality site architecture and effective SEO.

1. UX

User experience design, also referred to as UX, UED, or UXD, involves improving the accessibility and usability of a website in order to make the act of using a website as pleasurable as possible for the user or customer.

User Experience is an important part of website architecture.

It is just as or more important than the aesthetic appeal of your website. After all, a good looking website is pointless if it cannot be used effortlessly by the customer/user.

Your user must be able to interact with the website.

For instance, if you have an e-commerce site, then the site must be organized perfectly and be able to guide customers through the purchase process without confusing them or wasting their time.

So, how does this affect SEO?

Well, the answer to that is quite obvious and we have discussed this before. It's not enough to have keywords to make your site rank higher. You also need the right number of visitors and those visitors must be turned into repeat users/customers. One of the ways to make sure your customers/users are loyal to you is to provide a high quality user experience.

As they say, the first impression is the best impression. In a world where time is money, customers do not have the patience to even handle the slightest interference and difficulty. So, make sure your website is designed to be efficient and streamlined.

2. Page Speed

Page speed refers to the speed at which a particular web page loads; not to be confused with site speed, which refers to the speed at which the entire website loads. Page speed is measured in two ways – by determining the time taken for the entire page's content to be displayed or by determining the time taken by the browser to receive every byte from the web page.

However, all these measuring methods achieve the same – they tell you how fast your web page loads. The faster it loads, the better it is in terms of SEO.

Google's search algorithms are designed to rank websites according to site speed and also, page speed. In fact, studies have pointed out that Google uses the 'time to first byte' method in measuring page speed.

Plus, Google uses limited "crawl budgets", which means that if you have a slow loading web page, then Google will "crawl" only a few pages to stay in line with the crawl budget. This affects the way your site is indexed and in turn, your SEO.

Slow page speeds also affect UX. Studies have shown that websites with slow page speeds suffer from fewer conversion rates.

So, how do you improve page speed?

Well, there are certain measures you can take to increase page speed. For starters, you can try file compression. There are specific applications that compress JavaScript, HTML, and CSS files. You can also try using photo or image editing applications to compress the size of photos and other graphical elements of your website.

Another idea is to optimize your web page's code by removing unnecessary characters. You must also eliminate formatting, code comments, or unused code.

Finally, you can also reduce the number of redirects. Every time one page redirects to another, the user or customer has to wait longer for the HTTP request and response cycle.

3. Easy To Crawl

As you already know, search engines "crawl" the internet in search of websites and they "crawl" each website page. This is the method they use to index (make copies) your website. So, every time a user conducts a search, the search engine "crawls" the indexed pages to look for relevant content.

However, sometimes, there are certain things that can affect this "crawling" ability that search engines possess. For instance, if you run JavaScript or Flash, then there is a chance that your links can become invisible or hidden and invisible links result in pages getting missed, along with the content on those pages.

There is also something known as a "crawl budget". A "crawl

budget" refers to the specific amount of time or number of pages that a search engine is allowed to crawl per day. This budget is also relative to the authority and trust a site has.

Some major sites improve crawl efficiency by creating emphasis over specific pages. For instance, using internal link structures, robots.txt or establishing certain URL parameters to prevent unnecessary crawling are some of the methods sites use to boost crawl efficiency.

HTML and XML site maps are also useful in improving your site's "crawlability".

4. Duplicate Content

Duplicate content causes a lot of problems for search engines. When a search engine finds content that is virtually the same across multiple pages, it ends up having a hard time trying to figure out which page should be returned as a search result.

Plus, this problem gets worse when multiple users start linking different pages with the same content.

This causes a distortion in the value of the page that is being linked to. So, the bottom line is to ensure that each page has unique content to offer or to have one page with the content you want to focus on.

Duplicate pages can be created unknowingly. For instance, some sites have an entire non-www version instead of just using a redirect.

So, in order to avoid this scenario, you will have to use rel=canonical tags, pagination strategies, 301 redirects, and URL parameters.

5. Mobile Friendliness

It's the age of all things mobile and if your site isn't mobile-friendly, you're going to have a problem. In fact, Google rewards higher rankings to sites that are mobile friendly. Bing does this as well.

This is because mobile searches account for a huge part of the internet search traffic numbers.

So, if you're interested in improving your search engine rankings, make sure your site is optimized for mobile access. This is good for rankings and you will tap into a huge customer base. Mobile web users are a growing population and it has been predicted that they will overtake your average user who accesses the internet from the laptop or desktop.

You call also develop specific apps for your business and use app indexing and linking to drive traffic.

6. Keywords And URLs

There's a saying among SEO professionals and it goes like this – "The best URLs have keywords". It doesn't get truer than this. Keywords in the URL have a huge impact on your SEO. In fact, many e-commerce sites that boast of a high performance in organic search results use this strategy.

Using keywords in URLs is an effective way to provide users with some information on what they can expect to find on your site. It's like providing a thumbnail preview for a larger image.

Search engines can crawl URLs as long as they are linked to from another source (backlinks). A long time ago, URLs with category or product numbers, along with subdirectories and directories posed a challenge for search engines. This is not the case anymore.

Plus, keywords in the URL provide the relevance that search engines are looking for. They tell search engines about the kind of content on the page. Added to that, users are bound to click URLs if they have relevant keywords in them.

All in all, the end result here is that your website gets clicked on and the more it is clicked on, the higher your rankings go.

7. HTTPS and SSL

HTTPS refers to "Hypertext Transfer Protocol Secure" and SSL refers to "Secure Sockets Layer".

Here, SSL is an internet protocol that offers secure

communication via the internet either by encrypting data or authenticating a website. In the former method, data is secured and hidden from hackers while it is being transmitted. In the latter method, an SSL certificate functions like an ID and tells the browser that the site is exactly what it claims to be and that it's not fraudulent.

HTTPS, on the other hand, is a type of security protocol that is added to the SSL protocol. It is basically a way to add SSL security capabilities to standard HTTP based internet communication.

Now, these security features can affect your SEO because search engines like Google have actually established policies that rank SSL/HTTPs enabled sites higher.

This is a measure introduced by Google to improve internet security.

CHAPTER 7

Basic Elements Of Off-Page SEO: Trust

Google's search algorithms have undergone tremendous change over the past few years.

One of the most important changes that came with the Hummingbird update was 'Google Trust'. As the term obviously implies, trust has now become a major factor in helping Google determine how to rank a website and push it up in the organic search result rankings.

So, how does this work?

Well, if you were to go on Google and enter the search terms "make money online", you will find that the search results actually return links to articles instead of actual websites. What that means is that these articles are ranked higher than actual sites that might be optimized to match the search terms you entered. In other words, Google has identified these articles to be way more trustworthy than entire websites.

In other words, your SEO depends on the kind of "trust" you create around your website. Google, now, looks at a combination of multiple factors to determine how trustworthy your site is. So, if there is a lot of trust for your site, your site will rank higher on particular searches.

So, what factors affect trust in terms of offsite-SEO?

1. **Quality Links**

Well, one of the first things that affect a site's trust is actually a major deal in off-site SEO already. Yes. We're talking about quality backlinks. It doesn't take a rocket scientist to get this. If a trusted or authoritative website links back to yours, it simply boosts your reputation.

Quality backlinks are a great way to build your website's trust. However, collecting such links is easier said than done.

There are several strategies that you need to use. For starters, you will have to create quality content. High quality content will be read by people and will eventually get shared one way or another. This will boost your reputation and generally improve the way your site is perceived by users/ customers.

The second way to generate quality backlinks is to actually publish useful guest blogs. There are several blog sites that are willing to publish content written by you. However, you will need to produce quality content here too. Nobody wants to read just another blog. Make sure what you write is interesting, useful, relevant, and informative.

In fact, some blog-sites won't even publish your content if they feel it lacks quality.

Publishing quality content in the form of guest blogs has always been a reliable way to boost off-site SEO results. Many small-businesses have seen their rankings go up even with just a single guest blog publication.

When other authoritative sites start to pick up your guest blog, it's automatically going to link back to you and eventually, you will begin to gain that trust. Gone are the days when any backlink would do to keep the rankings climbing. Today, who shares your content matters just as much as the quality of your content.

Even if you publish a brilliant blog, it's not going to be useful until some authoritative website picks it up and links it back to you.

Plus, low quality backlinks can actually attract penalties and hurt your rankings.

2. **Bounce rate**

Bounce rate, as far as SEO goes, is a horrible thing. So, what does bounce rate mean? Well, bounce rate refers to the numbers of website visitors who leave your website after just looking at one page. A high bounce rate indicates that there is something wrong with your website and causes Google to lose trust with your site.

What causes a high bounce rate? The answer to this question is "anything or all". As in, it could literally be anything that's bothering your visitors or everything.

Maybe the content is poor or maybe the page speed is low. Maybe the navigation is confusing or maybe the overall UX is poor. Whatever it is, a high bounce rate isn't good for building trust.

So, make sure you prevent this from happening.

Studies have shown that lack of information or improperly organized information is one of the top causes of high bounce rates. In other words, when a customer fails to have expectations met immediately, they are going to "bounce". In order to avoid this, your content needs to be engaging. You need to ensure that you do not mislead the customer and that you always meet their expectations. Customer engagement is one of the best ways to avoid high bounce rates.

The next step is to promote your brand or indulge in brand storytelling. Tell your customer what you are and what you represent. Tell them what you have to offer.

One of the ways in which you can do this is by becoming more active on social media. Social media has turned into a one stop shop for people to know more about a particular brand.

By presenting your brand on social media, you are motivating the customer to get to know more about your brand.

Studies have indicated that 50 percent of visitors are bouncers. What that means is that half the users visiting your pages are bouncing off and never coming back. Various on-site and off-site SEO strategies are definitely useful in boosting traffic and improving engagement. But, today's customer spends a lot of time on social media. This makes social media a great platform for engaging with customers.

Most importantly, it reduces bounce rates. How you ask? Well, you can choose to present content selectively through social media. For instance, posting a link to a blog on your website will improve the click rate.

Your potential customers won't have to navigate an entire website to get to that particular blog. This way you will discourage them from bouncing and still manage to get enough views on your page.

To put it simply, get the content directly to your customer instead of expecting them to come to your website, only to get confused and leave.

Finally make sure your website has an optimized design and delivers a great UX. For example, make sure the navigation is seamless. Don't force your customer to think too much about what to click next. The process must be intuitive.

Be clear with your CTA and purpose. Confused visitors are the ones who bounce the most.

Implement responsive design so that your website can be accessed across multiple platforms. This will increase traffic and make the UX even better.

3. Domain Age

Domain age is nothing but the age of your website and it has a fair bit to do with creating trust. The older your website is, the more trust it tends to build for itself. Domain age is measured in two ways – the duration of its existence since registration and the duration of its activity in the context of possessing crawlable content.

Search engines measure domain age by looking at the first time the website was crawled and its inbound links were noticed.

Domain age plays a small role in SEO. Since, search engines work towards providing valuable results, one of the "trust" factors they look at is domain age. An old website is considered to have longevity, which is an indicator of quality.

However, it is not the most important factor that builds trust. As a website owner, you will still have to build a reputation through other off-site SEO strategies such as publishing high quality content and generating quality backlinks.

There is a myth being perpetuated that sites with an older domain age tend to be favoured by search engines.

However, this is a gross misconception. Domain age provides more of an added advantage. It is not a stand-alone factor that affects trust. In order to gain trust, sites still need to rely on quality content and backlinks.

New sites tend to be affected by domain age not because they are new, but because they do not have the right content to attract attention yet.

This affects the way the site is indexed, in turn causing it to suffer from low rankings.

However, there is a solution. All one needs to do is start adding high quality, SEO optimized content to overcome the domain age issue.

Once the content keeps flowing in, the site will begin to gradually garner attention.

After a point, domain age stops being a problem.

In fact, domain age has always been an insignificant indicator of a site's trustworthiness.

Its effect on SEO, from an overall perspective, is minimal at best.

4. **Site Identity**

The identity of your website also affects the trust factor of your site. Is your site exactly what it claims to be?

As we discussed earlier, Google ranks SSL certified sites higher because it is easier to determine the identity of these sites.

So, in order to build trust, search engines need to know the identity behind your website.

This simply means that you will have to implement strict security measures to make sure your site is safe to use.

This will also help visitors gain some confidence in your site.

CHAPTER 8

Basic Elements of Off-Page SEO: Links

What Exactly Is A Backlink?

A backlink is an incoming link to a webpage. Backlinks can be considered as relationships among webpages, allowing users to explore different pages on the internet. Previously, backlinks were an important metric influencing the ranking of webpages. SEO professionals focused on increasing backlinks to rank higher on major search engines. Though incoming/inbound links help with optimization, their quality matters more than their number.

How Do Backlinks Assist With Optimization?

There are multiple advantages to creating backlinks to your webpages. One is faster site indexing. Backlinks help search engine spiders discover links to your website and crawl it effectively. If yours is a new website, backlinks can be useful in the quicker discovery and indexing of sites.

Another advantage of backlinks is the amount of referral traffic it brings. This referral traffic is targeted and has a low bounce rate.

Factors To Consider When Getting Backlinks

Quality Of Links

Google views backlinks as a sign of authority. A simple example of a quality backlink is when the one pointing from another site to yours is relevant to your site's content. The greater the relevance, the higher the quality of the backlink.

Different Ways To Get Backlinks

1. Be active on social media: Engaging on social media is all about sharing, tweeting, getting mentions and retweets, and creating a buzz around your brand. Backlinks are an important source of value gained from a strategic social media presence. Social shares can translate into a lot of backlinks for you, so it is vital to get the wheels of your content marketing campaign in motion.

As you keep creating useful, share-worthy content, and repositioning old content, you must simultaneously start putting it before readers. Post links to every article that you post on social platforms, and to relevant LinkedIn groups that you're a member of. Submit your posts to StumbledUpon and Reddit. Even posts that get just a few upvotes on these sites can fetch you hundreds of visitors, and multiply backlinking opportunities.

2. Create infographics: Infographics continue to be one of the most popular content formats shared online. They present data in digestible chunks for easy consumption. Creatively designed infographics make dry statistics appealing to the eye and encourage reading and sharing. Capitalize on their potential by creating infographics that your audience will find useful. Put them to work on your blog and social media pages to earn backlinks.

3. Get reviews from bloggers: Here's where influencer marketing can tie into your link-building efforts. If you have made efforts to engage key individuals (bloggers, YouTube stars, and authority/popular voices with a strong and loyal following on social media) to promote your brand, they can also help you grow quality backlinks.

Create a list of serious, influential bloggers. Offer them your product for free. When reaching out to them via email or other means, don't ask for a review or a link, as this is a violation of Google's Webmaster Guidelines. Send them your product and leave it to them to decide whether or not they want to feature it on their blog.

4. Reclaim links: When your product or service earns a mention in a blog, there is a possibility that the blogger may not have linked to you. Don't let it remain a missed opportunity. Contact the blogger via email and remind him/her to add your link.

You'll first need to find unlinked mentions of your brand, and there are several online – free ones included – that you can use. BuzzSumo, Mention.net and RankTank are some options to try. The tools let you know when someone writes about you online. You can then check if they have linked back to your site, and if they haven't, request the necessary additions.

Anchor Text

Anchor text is the clickable text in a hyperlink. It is added within website content, which when clicked by visitors, directs them to another page.

Example of an anchor text :

<a href ="http://www.seodigital.com">New York digital marketing agency</a>.

But users see only the clickable part of the anchor text.

- <a> and </a> are the beginning and end of the link tag respectively

- http://www.seodigital.com is the link referral location

- 'digital marketing agency' is the anchor text

Anchor text is a relevancy signal along with the meta title, heading tags and surrounding text. Optimizing anchor text involves adding the keywords related to your target search terms.

For instance, if your digital marketing agency is located in New York, and social media marketing is one of your main services, you can create anchor texts quite easily.

On your Home Page, you can use internal links or text links to describe all your digital marketing services. One of these will be 'social media marketing', and this term can be the anchor text. You can similarly create texts out of the various services you offer, say 'SEO' and 'Pay-per-click advertising'.

Avoid adding zero anchor texts, such as 'click here...'.

Also avoid using the same anchor text multiple times, or Google bots will view it as a manipulation of the keyword phrase.

There are different types of anchor text as listed below:

- Zero anchor text: As mentioned above, zero anchor text like 'Click here' does not have any significant link value.

- Exact match anchor text: Many instances of exact match anchor text may be perceived as unnatural link building.

- Naked URLs: A naked URL is a hyperlink for which the anchor text is the URL itself or some variation of it.

- Partial match anchor text: You can use just the key phrase instead of the targeted key phrase, 'website development' instead of 'New York website development'. Search engine spiders can crawl the surrounding text to figure out that you're talking about a website development in New York.

- Hybrid anchor text: You can also use a combination of anchor texts directly related to your brand with non-branded phrases.

How To Avoid Unnatural Links?

- You may repeat anchor texts across your guest blogs or copy-paste your biography or directory entry when submitting to guest blogs or directories. As mentioned previously, Google may view them as unnatural, repetitive or duplicate links. Just vary the content a bit and you'll be good to go.

- Use synonyms; for instance, replace 'digital marketing agency' with 'digital marketing company' or 'digital marketing firm'.

- Use singular or plural forms; for instance, 'XYZ is one of the most trusted digital marketing agencies..'

- Combine keywords; for instance, 'website design agency and SEO company'

- Use keyword modifiers; for instance, 'digital marketing agency in New York' or 'New York digital marketing agency'.

- Use different anchor texts to link to one URL

Contextual Links

A contextual link is found within the body of the content and matches the context of the idea surrounding the link.

It can be natural – a link from another website – or artificial – a link back to one of your blog posts or product pages.

Besides earning you backlinks, contextual links help increase brand awareness and boost website traffic. Linking out to authoritative sites is a reliable way of enhancing brand credibility and encouraging readers to return and share. By improving reader experience through contextual link building, you can also make a favorable impression on Google and improve your PageRank.

When linking out, you want to prioritize top-notch content that makes readers glad that they took the time to read it.

One example of linkbait content is an article that has gone viral, and whose popularity is evident by top page positions in search. Another is long-form content that discusses a topic in detail and provides substantial value to the readers. Look at domain experts and top blogs in your niche for top-of-the-line long-form content.

A third is infographics; many provide the HTML code to allow you to republish to your site with a link back to the original. In this regard, you can use an SEO strategy called 'Guestographics'.

Here's how it works: offer publishers free and unique infographics relevant to their site; customize the introduction to the infographic. Publishers won't ignore the opportunity to share ready-to-go content. It's a simple yet effective way to earn more views, shares and contextual backlinks.

Number Of Links

The number of backlinks you can get also matter. Before you start exploring backlinking strategies, take a fresh look at your website to assess if your content is well-organized, navigation is easy, and the information you provide is relevant and useful to the sites that will link to your website.

When you start producing content, wait for it to be indexed by Google, and then start building quality links.

If you start generating links to new content very quickly, Google may find it manipulative. An easy way to get your context indexed is to add your website URL on Alexa – which Google spiders are constantly crawling – and check the metrics.

Alexa adds new, optimized pages to its database. When Google crawls Alexa the next time, they will pick up your new content.

CHAPTER 9

Basic Elements of Off-page SEO: Personal Factors

As the name suggests, these relate to the person(s) of your intended audience, hence 'personal'.

These are factors that do not really have anything to do with the content on the page itself, or anything that might have been embedded in them.

Country

If you notice, the search results for a particular query that are shown are relevant to the country one is located in, unless it is something that has universal appeal (like information) and is not restricted by geographical boundaries.

If you type in www.google.com in the address bar of your browser, you are usually redirected to a country specific domain. Like say, if you were in the United Kingdom, you would be automatically redirected to www.google.co.uk.

There are some 200 country-specific Google domains, and the only exception seems to be the United States, which is served by www.google.com.

So how does Google know which country you are in? It gleans this information from a number of factors, like your Internet Service Provider (it is your ISP that determines your IP address, and the country of the ISP known as IP addresses are allocated accordingly and not at random) – there are small things like 'cookies' which store this information.

What it means for you is that depending on the country of a user, your site could be displayed on the very first page itself, or somewhere further down the order, where it is unlikely to be seen at all. You can check this out for yourself – if you query 'mobile phone' on www.google.co.uk and www.google.co.in, you are bound to be served up with different results.

OK, so maybe there is something that causes British websites to show up first on www.google.co.uk and Indian websites to show up first in www.google.co.in. These are country specific sites after all. You could try the same experiment with Bing, which does not have country-specific sites and you would see that the search results are local to your country (the country where you got your domain registered)

So it is a bit of a downer if someone overseas does not see your website at all, and you were hoping for international business, but then again, keep in mind that it is only for generic search terms, like 'best leather sofa'. Someone who keys in your company's name and country would definitely get the link to your site.

On the brighter side, customers in your own country are better if you don't want to be bothered with foreign exchange, shipping, and import/export regulations for something like the above. Now if you were a bank in the Cayman Islands, and your target audience was not the local population, but say wealthy Americans, it is better to get your domain registered in the United States. What if you were a private Swiss banker and you wanted a multi-country audience? Well, that would relate to on-page SEO – there are a lot of things that could be embedded in the HTML of your site.

In short, one way would be to have multiple languages for your site, like Wikipedia. But we know translation fees are expensive, and it could achieve the opposite effect if there was an error in translation; or the translation has a different meaning in that country.

Remember how Kentucky Fried Chicken's 'Finger-lickin' good' slogan misfired when the Chinese translation, although accurate, had the meaning of 'Eat your fingers off' among the local population?

Pepsi's 'Come Alive' tagline, another phrase that was translated correctly, meant 'Pepsi makes your ancestors come back from the dead' among the Chinese.

Another way is to have multiple country-specific domains, like www.abc.com, www.abc.de, www.abc.fr and so on. But then again, this too is expensive and all domain name and extension combinations might not always be available.

In such an instance, you could try having country-specific pages on the same site, like en.abc.com, fr.abc.com, de.abc.com. A better way of achieving the same effect would be to have sub-directories like www.abc.com/en, www.abc.com/fr and www.abc.com/de

Googlebots crawl through the HTML content on your page, and even if there is only one language, say English, you could still indicate that there are no alternates for those who use a different version of English.

```
<link     rel="alternate"     href="http://abc.com/en-ie" hreflang="en-ie">
<link rel="alternate" href="http://abc.com/en-ca" hreflang="en-ca">
<link rel="alternate" href="http://abc.com/en-au" hreflang="en-au">
<link rel="alternate" href="http://abc.com/en" hreflang="en">
```

This code actually ensures that your page, written in American English, will be shown to an Australian whose language is Australian English. This is another way of ensuring a more global audience for your webpage with minimal effort.

City

If you look more closely, the search results are shown specific to the city of the user. Those in the same city as you or located close to your city are likely to see your site listed on the very first page itself. Somebody looking for 'good Asian restaurants' would be served up with local restaurants that serve Asian cuisine.

Again, if you provide accurate business information, Google also displays your contact phone number(s) and hours of operation, in addition to showing where it is located, using Google Maps.

There is again the same dilemma – what do you do if you serve a nationwide population and need those residing in other cities to see your website/page? This too has to do more with on-page SEO and there are various hacks that can be employed to ensure that you show up as a top leather sofa manufacturer even if someone in another city queried for 'best leather sofa'.

Search History

If the search engine user has visited your site before (this is known from the cookies; or if you are logged into Google, it keeps a record of your recent search history), Google might think that your site/page is relevant and display it among the top results. You might have noticed when you signed into Google, it populates your search terms based on what you queried for in the past.

So if you Googled for 'best ways to make a difference in society', that might be presented as an auto-fill option when you just type in 'best ways to' (this time your intention might be search for 'best ways to mingle with others at a wedding reception', but Google is constantly learning – this will be presented as another auto-fill option the next time you simply type in 'best' with another query in mind).

Social Media

If you own a YouTube channel for your site/brand/product/

service or a social media profile on say Facebook, Twitter, Google+ or Pinterest, more 'likes' translates into a higher ranking for your website and you are more likely to be seen at the top in the search results. So it makes sense to get on to social media. On every social media platform, there are people who are termed 'Influencers'.

They are experts, or perceived as such, and they are widely followed on social media. Google knows who the influencers are, and them liking or sharing your website/page counts for a lot more than the average user.

In terms of numbers, influencers sharing a link to your page (all links are seen separately by Google, so www.abc.com/whitehatseo is different from www.abc.com/blackhatseo but rest assured that www.abc.com benefits out of this) also has a ripple effect – their followers are likely to visit the page (and perhaps the home page and other pages as well), and the increased traffic boosts your page's rankings. Followers of influencers may also choose to like or share the same link, which further increases the chances of your page appearing on the first page.

So you see how it is not just quantity that matters, but also the quality of the likes/shares on social media. Don't think about 'buying' likes for your page. Google is continuously evolving, updating its search algorithms (first there was Panda in 2011, then Penguin in 2012 and Hummingbird in 2013) to weed out those who try to fool it.

If you are blacklisted, recovering could be harder than trying to achieve organic growth. Google does tend to penalize such websites, so it is better not to try anything of the sort.

There are many ways you can engage with users on social media – all these are covered in the next chapter.

CHAPTER 10

Basic Elements Of Off-page SEO: Social Media

Social media is a great way of improving off-page SEO. The mere fact that people are talking about something is proof of their interest. We have already seen how the quality of 'likes' and 'shares' improves a page's rankings and has a greater impact than the quantity (number of 'likes' and 'shares'). Now how exactly do you get an influencer to 'like' or 'share' your link in the first place? One way of growth hacking (this is the name given to it) is to quote the influencer as an expert on the topic – this directly increases the chances of the influencer liking and sharing your link.

How To Engage With Customers / Users On Social Media

As always, content is king.

It was king, and will probably continue to be so. The sooner you realize this, the better.

Facebook

You need to first set up a company page/profile and most importantly, link your website to it. But merely doing this will not automatically ensure a steady stream of likes. Even if it did, you still need content for others to like and share.

On Facebook, a contribution by you to the community is

termed a post. What exactly do you 'post'? A post can be text-based, or there could be multimedia associated with it, like an image, a collection of images or a video. You could have multimedia-only posts, but it helps to add a short description (even if it is only a one-liner) that explains what the multimedia is about.

A combination of both text and multimedia works best – this is twelve times as likely to be shared than text-only posts.

The images have to be striking enough to grab eyeballs – most users are going to see it in their feeds, as opposed to them coming to your page to check out new posts. A relevant image guarantees that there is a 94% greater chance of your post being seen by users. Photography plays an important role here – high shutter-speed photography images are popular among Facebook users.

Even if that is not applicable to your product or service, aesthetically pleasing photographs are always a good bet. One clothing company managed to get attention with a picture of a woman in a red dress having fun shopping – given that Facebook's theme is blue, this stood out in user feeds.

Multiple images are good, but keep in mind that Facebook typically tends to shows the first one the largest. The sizes of the others are reduced, and their appeal (the overall appeal of the post as well) may be lost on the user. Infographics (people love information, and those willing to share information with them) are also 'liked' and 'shared' three times more than any other form of content.

Always make sure that there is a link to your website or page included in the post.

Facebook now has hashtags for trending topics. You could take advantage of the interest generated in the topic or subject by posting something relevant from your website or page and including the hashtag.

Twitter

Twitter is known for being the social media platform where you have only 140 characters of text to express what you want to say. While this is extremely limiting, Twitter allows you to add images or a six-second video as part of your 'tweet'. If you would like to include a longer video, it might have to be uploaded on YouTube or some other site (perhaps even your own) and the link to it mentioned. A video thumbnail that gets included automatically ensures that people who see the tweet understand the link is to a video.

You can have a 140-character long (this is the maximum allowed; it can also be shorter than this) text-only tweet, or this can be supplemented by multimedia. A tweet that is accompanied by an image or video has a 313% more engagement rate than text alone. Such tweets are also retweeted 52% more than the ones without visual content. Include a short Vine video, which can be of six seconds duration at the most, to the text and enjoy a 250% higher engagement rate with users of Twitter.

Even with the text, there are hacks to improve user engagement (always see to it that there is a link to your page or site with the text)

- **Exclamation marks:** These improve the engagement rate by 43%

- **Referencing other Twitter users:** These tweets which contain @ have a 51% more engagement rate than those without them (the higher the celebrity status of the Twitter user referenced, the greater is likelihood of the engagement rate for the tweet)

- **Hashtags:** These cause user engagement to rise by 122% on an average. For a trending topic, the user engagement is bound to be much higher.

- **Include numbers:** Facts and figures that are easily

understood can improve the user engagement rate of a tweet by 17%.

Diane von Fürstenberg, a fashion designer, got on to Twitter and saw traffic to her site increasing by 13%.

She now has close to a million followers on the social media platform and gets nearly 20,000 views a day for her website. This might not be large, but it is definitely significant when catering to an upper segment of the population.

As proof to show how much of an impact influencers can have, von Fürstenberg's following was only 22,000 in 2010, but this included many influencers – it is they who have caused her following to rise by so much in just six years.

YouTube

One of the fastest growing companies in the world, RevZilla, started out of an apartment with just $30,000 in capital.

They are now worth $75 million and credit their success to using YouTube, where they visually demonstrate their products – motorcycle parts, helmets and accessories. Their website gets over a 100,000 views per day.

Why you should consider using YouTube is because video consumption has been increasing, and this is aided by better internet speeds and the proliferation of powerful, mobile devices (30-50% of all internet access happens on such devices).

Google+

This is Google's own social media platform and functions very much like all the others.

You can publish content (text only; with an accompanying image or video; or the image/video alone). Here, a '+1' is the equivalent of a 'like' on Facebook. Whatever social media activity occurs on Google+ is indexed by Google immediately, and so theoretically, it should be the best for generating traffic for your website.

The reason why it isn't is because not everyone has a Google account. But it is still a good way of improving off-page SEO and whatever rules apply to content on other social media is relevant here as well.

LinkedIn

This is a social media platform, but not for those looking to relax or de-stress. It is a professional networking site, and you can drive traffic to your own website by publishing quality articles that carry a link to your page/website. You can include images, but what would be better are infographics – these have a 300% greater chance of being 'liked' and 'shared'.

Remember that those on LinkedIn are not here to 'have fun'. They mostly access the site at work and have very limited time to spend on each 'update' (this is the equivalent of a post/tweet on Facebook/Twitter respectively) – this is perhaps the reason why videos are not shared much on LinkedIn.

Instagram

This is a mobile application which allows users to share images and video on social media platforms like Facebook, Twitter, Flickr and Tumblr. Originally, it allowed the sharing of photographs only in a square shape or 1:1 aspect ratio, where the height equals the width (this meant that 4:3 and 16:9 aspect ratio photographs would be cropped); but this was done away with in August 2015.

It now has 400 million users globally and those using it to communicate with millions of followers include Victoria Beckham, Louis Vuitton and Chanel.

It is great for brand building and hence generating interest in your site (people would then search for your company and come to your site), but if you want more immediate results, all you have to do is include the URL to your site/page in the photographs that you publish. It is a good practice to include your company name and logo in all the photographs.

Instagram is now owned by Facebook, so its reach is wider than you think.

Pinterest

Pinterest is a photo sharing website. 'Pins' or images can be organized by collections known as 'boards'.

This social media platform is frequented by those to whom visual media – specifically, still photographs – appeals, so your images have to be really striking if they are to increase traffic to your website or page and improve off-page SEO. The same guidelines apply as in the case of Instagram.

To sum up in a single line:

Using social media judiciously can work wonders for your website by aiding off-page SEO greatly and must be part of your plans.

CHAPTER 11

Local SEO

Get Registered On Local Directories And Websites

This can be a great way of driving traffic to your site. Also, the more mentions of your name there are online, the greater is your name indexed (this is good for the rankings as well). With the proliferation of local directories, it becomes hard to figure out on which site it is good to be listed. But the answer is notoriously simple – the ones with the most traffic.

The logic is plain and relatively straightforward, if a local directory has a large number of users, the chances of people viewing your listing and contacting you or visiting your website is greater than a local directory which has only a small number of users.

For Google, there is Google My Business.

The first step is having a dedicated website (not a business page on a larger platform that also has pages of other businesses). Google also asks you to list your place on Google Maps. This can be hard for those running home businesses and do not want customers visiting them in person, but this is Google's way of establishing that you do exist in the real world and are not some virtual company.

Then you are also expected to set up a Google+ page for your business, with photos. Updating it regularly earns you bonus points with Google, and there is even more to be had if the content is of exceptionally great quality that the people you connect with '+1' it (this is the equivalent of 'like' on Facebook). Adding accurate information about your business (like contact numbers, working hours etc.) only aids in greater discovery of your business/site.

And of course, you need to respond to users who review your business.

Although Google is the top search engine (65% of all searches worldwide), there are also people who use Bing and Yahoo!

20% of searches happen with Bing, and Yahoo! accounts for 12%. Both Bing and Yahoo! have local business listings and you could list your business and website on these portals as well. Will Google, Bing and Yahoo! do? No, there is also Facebook (it now lists businesses) and LinkedIn. Pinterest and Instagram are other two social media sites where you could list your business and website, and then there is also the classic Yellow Pages which has gone online.

There is also Yelp, White Pages, Foursquare and many others. Check which have listings of local businesses in your area and get yours listed as well.

Most of them are free, and so it doesn't really cost you anything, except your time. But doing this could also go a long way towards getting more traffic for your site, and increased earnings in the process.

Include Your Location On Your Social Media Profiles

As mentioned earlier, this is a way of verifying that yours is not a 100% online company and that you can indeed be found in the real world. Google has Google Maps and Bing has Bing Maps. A lot of other applications use either of these two (Facebook now uses maps from Here), and so the address (including this might be optional, but which customer would want to deal with if you don't have a physical mailing address?

Doesn't any company with just an email and a phone number seem shady to you?) being backed by a real-time location on social media profiles is unbeatable when it comes to credibility.

Not just to customers, but also to search engines – the legal implications aside, it is bad for their own reputation if someone deals with a business whose website they served up in response to a query, and loses his money in the process.

Get Reviews From Local Customers

Reviews and ratings from real people (if you notice, on Google their pictures are also displayed alongside their reviews – this cannot be replicated by bots) further bolster your credibility of being a real business. This impacts your rankings, and the link to your website is likely to be displayed higher than the link to another website which does not have reviews or ratings, when both are served up in response to a particular query.

Because this rating and reviewing is integrated on Google, anyone can review and rate your company by either entering the name of your business into the search bar so that your business's information comes up on the right side and then clicking on the 'Write a review'; or doing the same after zeroing in on your physical location on Google Maps. How this helps is that the more positive reviews and higher ratings you get, your business (replete with its website) is ranked higher.

So when someone queries for 'Best Thai restaurants in New York', the ones that are top rated are shown first. Even among them, the ones that have more top ratings from real users are taken into account. This way, a restaurant that has an average rating of 4.3 stars out of five, but has more five-star ratings than another restaurant with an average rating of 4.5, but only a lesser number of five-star ratings from users, gets shown higher up when they are listed.

Not everyone may be a Google user. Some use Yelp to leave their reviews of your business. It works the same way here as well – those rated the higher are displayed ahead of those who are rated less than them.

Instead of waiting for customers to rate your business, you could nudge them to leave a review on Google or Yelp (this is where Bing pulls ratings from) when you present them with the bill with a line at the bottom, like

'Loved our service? Review us on Google'

The 'service' could be replaced by 'products' or anything more specific, but this is just a sample to indicate how you could theoretically get more reviews.

If you notice that your customers use Yelp more, you could replace Google with Yelp in the above statement. Yes, it opens the door to negative reviews too, but then again, there is an equal likelihood of you getting a positive review. If your treat your customers right, there are bound to be more positive reviews than negative ones.

As seen from the above New York Thai restaurant example, even if there are more four-star ratings than five-star ratings, the bulk of them together work out better than a handful of five-star ratings alone – so you needn't worry about being rated poorly and that pulling down your website's ranking/local business listing.